Introduction

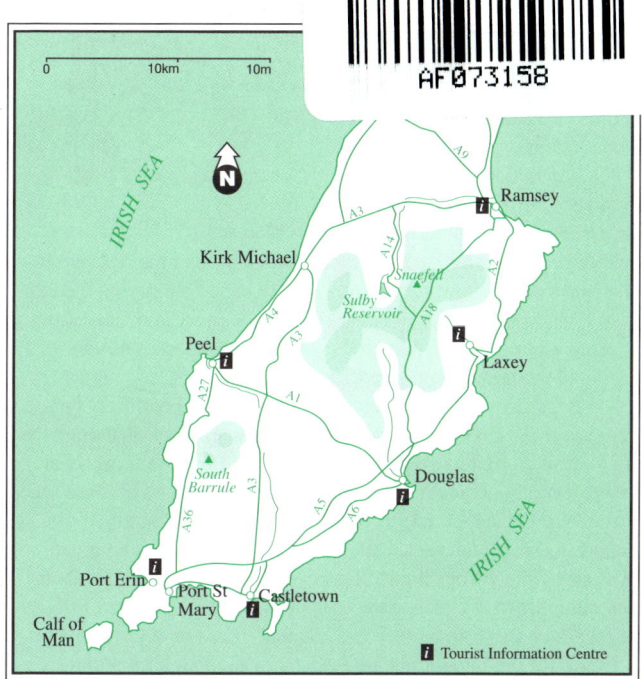

The Isle of Man is a unique and fascinating corner of the British Isles. Most people will know something about it – its famous three-legged insignia, TT racing, cats with no tails – but too few know about the variety and beauty of its landscape, or about the range and quality of its walking.

Let's start with the basics. The Isle of Man is an island in the Irish Sea, approximately equidistant from the shores of England, Scotland and Northern Ireland. It has a compact, regular shape and measures 32 miles from north-east to south-west and 14 miles at its broadest point. The interior of the island is comprised of hills and moorland – rising to 2,037ft/621m at its highest point (Snaefell – *Walk 10*) – with good farmland on the lower slopes and on the flat northern plain. There are scattered woods, but no significant forests; no large rivers, but a host of swift-flowing streams descending from the hills to the coast through deep, wooded glens.

Laxey Wheel (Walk 5)

The population of the island is around 85,000. Almost half of these live in the island's capital – Douglas – and the connected village of Onchan. The bulk of the rest live in the island's other major settlements – Laxey and Ramsey on the east coast; Peel on the west; and Port Erin, Port St Mary and Castletown in the south – but there are numerous smaller settlements throughout the island and the population is generally well spread.

The large number of settlements means a correspondingly large number of roads. Driving on the island is generally easy, though the side roads are often narrow and winding. Traffic tends to move at around 50mph – which is slightly odd, given that some of these roads are used for the annual Isle of Man TT races! (Incidentally, if you are uninterested in motorbikes, make sure you avoid the island in late-May/early-June.) You should also be aware that you will encounter large numbers of cyclists on the roads – and indeed on some hill tracks, where there are numerous mountain bikes (and trials bikes).

There is a full bus service on the island, and in addition to the roads there is a steam railway linking Douglas and Port Erin, an electric railway between Douglas and Ramsey, and another electric railway climbing Snaefell. Level crossings are a common feature on side roads, and due care must be taken.

Politically, the island is a self-governing crown dependency. What this means in practice is that, while the Queen is head of state, the island is not part of the United Kingdom and has never been a member of the EU. It has its own elected parliament (the Tynwald, which sits in Douglas), its own currency (the

The Triskelion

Manx pound – though visitors should note that this is held at parity with the pound sterling, and that UK bank notes are accepted as legal tender on the island), and its own flag (the triskelion – three armoured legs on a red background). It also has its own tax regime, and the obvious wealth of much of the Isle of Man is largely due to the individuals and companies attracted to the island by its low taxes. UK visitors will notice little practical difference on arriving on the island, but they should be aware that their mobile signal will automatically switch to one of the Isle of Man providers, and there may be roaming charges.

The island can be reached by car ferry from Heysham (all year), or Liverpool, Belfast and Dublin (summer only). There is also an airport on the island (at Castletown), with links to a number of British airports.

The Isle of Man has a history and culture too rich and complex to be dealt with in the space available here, but visitors will quickly become aware of the island's Celtic aspect. There is a Manx language (related to Irish and Scottish Gaelic), and although visitors are unlikely to hear it spoken (it almost died out, and is only now being rejuvenated), it will be encountered in place names and on road signs. There is also a link with the vikings, who controlled the island for several centuries. The splendid terraced waterfront at Douglas is a link with the island's tourist boom in the late-19th- and early-20th centuries. Major historical structures include the splendid Castle Rushen in Castletown *(21)*, the dramatic Peel Castle on its little island, reached by a causeway *(11,12)*, and the Laxey Wheel *(5)* – a massive, water-powered pump which is a splendid memorial to the island's mining heritage.

The walks on the island are plentiful, varied and of high quality – every corner of the island has its own personality, and the walks vary accordingly. For rough, cliff-top coastal walks, head down to the south-west of the island. The walks over Bradda Head *(18)* and around the headland

Peel Castle (Walks 11 & 12)

south-west of Port Erin and Port St Mary *(19,20)* provide rough walking and splendid views along the cliffs and down to the Calf of Man, off the southern end of the island. (Bird watchers should also look out for choughs – coastal crows with curved red beaks – on these west coast walks.)

There is slightly gentler cliff scenery south of Peel *(11,12)*, and around Port Grenaugh *(16,17)*, Port Soderick *(15)* and Maughold Head *(2)* on the east coast, while the coast walks at Point of Ayre *(1)* follow long beaches of sand and stone, backed by dunes and rough, rolling grassland.

For woodland, try the splendid Dhoon Glen *(3)*, Ballaglass Glen *(4)* or Glen Maye *(12,13)*: short, steep, narrow valleys full of trees, rocks and waterfalls, leading down to rocky, narrow beaches. If you prefer open viewpoints, the finest are the two west coast follies of Corrin's Tower *(11,12)* and Milner's Tower *(18)*, the low southern peak of South Barrule *(14)* (a short climb to a fine view), the long ridge of North Barrule *(9)* (overlooking Ramsey and the north of the island), and, of course, Snaefell *(10)*. In addition, there are fine high-level walks in the northern hills around Kirk Michael, Sulby and Sulby Reservoir *(6,7,8)*.

These routes make use of the island's rights of way and 'greenways' (essentially bridleways, which may be used by horse-riders, cyclists and motor cyclists). They are well signposted and shown on the OS 1:50,000 map of the island (plus the 1:25,000 map produced by the government and available on the island). In addition, walkers will encounter signs for long-distance paths. By far the most significant of these is the Raad ny Foillan (Manx for 'The Gull Road'): a 95 mile/150km coastal path around the entire island, but you may also see signs for the Millennium Way (Ramsey to Castletown) and Bayr ny Skeddan ('The Herring Way'), between Castletown and Peel.

We hope you will enjoy these routes. A quick look at the OS map will show you plenty more, and it is worthwhile making time for them. The walks of the Isle of Man deserve to be better known.

The Winkie, Point of Ayre (Walk 1)

1 Point of Ayre _____ C

Two walks along the beach, and through or behind the dunes, in the Nature Reserve at the northern tip of the island. Length: up to **8 miles/13km**; *Height Climbed:* None.

O.S. Sheet 95

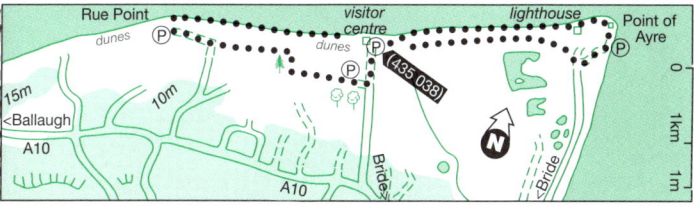

To reach the start of these walks, drive north from Ramsey on the A10. After 3 miles you pass through the village of Bride. Ignore junctions with the A17 and A16 and continue a further mile until a road heads right signposted for Ayres Visitors Centre.

This road runs straight towards the coast. After a mile the road becomes a track, and there is a car park in a clump of trees to the left. This is a possible start point for the walk to Rue Point. Either park here or continue to the car park by the visitor centre, behind the dunes at the end of the track, were there is also a wooden viewing tower.

Now you have a choice. **For the walk to the lighthouse on Point of Ayre**, simply head right from the end of the track – either along the beach or through the low dunes and grassland behind. Either way, you end up at the red and white striped lighthouse on the most northerly point of the island (1818).

Assuming you return to the car park, the total length of this walk is 4 miles/6.5km.

For the walk to Rue Point, walk back up the access track and turn right, onto the track leading into the car park in the stand of trees. Rather than edging right, into the parking area, keep straight on to reach a field gate. Beyond this, a clear, grassy track runs through gorse and grassland. There are occasional junctions, but there is no doubt about the route: just aim for a stand of conifers which quickly becomes visible ahead.

When you reach the conifers, turn right on the track down their near side. At the end of the trees you join a path running right to left along the bottom of the plantation. Turn left along this and follow the path to a car park behind the dunes.

Either return by the same route or walk through the dunes, onto the beach, and turn right. You will know you are level with the main car park when you see the wooden tower to your right.

The total distance of this walk is 4 miles/6.5km.

2 Port Lewaigue & Maughold Head _____ B

A walk along low cliffs following part of the Raad ny Foillan from the end of Ramsey Bay to the superb viewpoint of Maughold Head. Possible return by a quiet public road. **NB:** *The first section of this walk is not possible at high tide, so check tides before setting out.* Length: **2½ miles/4km** (one way); *Height Climbed:* **350ft/100m**.   *O.S. Sheet 95*

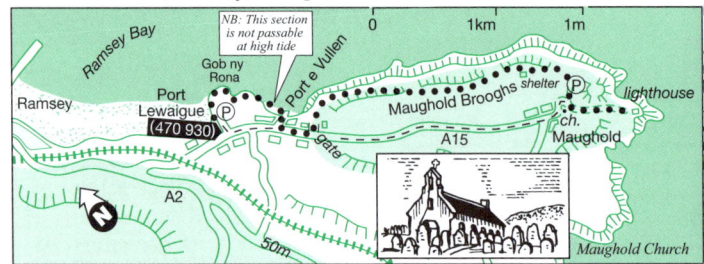

Maughold Church

To reach the start of this walk, follow the A2/A15 south from Ramsey. Just after a blue crossing, look for the blue marker for the Raad ny Foillan (coastal path) to the left of the road. Follow this down a tarred lane to a car park above Port Lewaigue, from where there are fine sea views.

Look for the start of a grassy path running round the edge of the bay behind a low stone wall. Follow this round the headland of Gob ny Rona to reach the houses at Port e Vullen. The path ends at a flight of steps. Drop down these and on to the beach (**N.B.** if the tide is high, return to the car park and follow the A15 to Port e Vullen instead).

Walk to the public slipway then follow the road beyond up to a junction. Go left (sign) and continue by the side of the road. As you leave the houses, look for a kissing gate to the left of the road (Maughold Brooghs). Go through this and follow the clear narrow path beyond.

The path (wet in places) continues around the headland through bracken and gorse. At the high point, you pass a shelter and beyond this views to the east and south open up.

The path eventually drops down through a kissing gate to reach a grassy car park. Follow the entrance track to the car park to reach a metalled road. Turn left to reach the lighthouse at Maughold Head.

Return to the entrance to the car park, but now continue a short distance to reach the entrance to the churchyard (fine display of early gravestones and Celtic crosses). From here, either return by the coast or (for a shorter route) walk on through the churchyard, and the village beyond, and follow the A15.

3 Dhoon Glen _____ B

A short, steep walk down one of the finest of the island's wooded glens. The views of the waterfall are dramatic, but please be aware that there are a great many steps on this walk. Length: **1½ miles/2.5km**; *Height Climbed:* **580ft/180m**.

O.S. Sheet 95

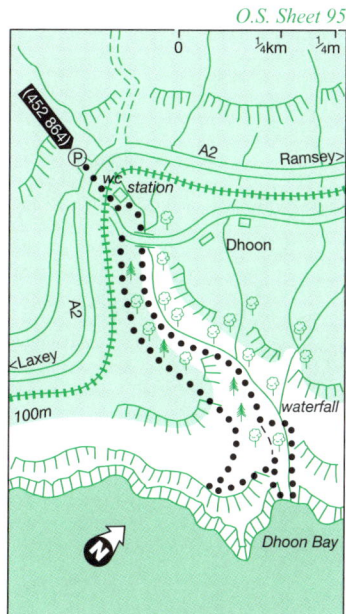

Drive 2 miles north from Laxey, on the A2, and park in a large car park to the left of the road, on the outside of a tight bend.

Cross the road and the railway beyond (carefully) to reach the building at Dhoon Glen Station. Take the path/steps to the right of the building, then turn left below it. A sequence of paths and steps now leads down into a wooded tributary glen. The path runs down this glen then passes under a minor road through a tunnel.

Beyond this the clear path continues down the main glen through mature woodland. When the path splits, go left. A series of flights of steps zig-zags down to the floor of the narrow glen, until you are looking up at a fine, forked waterfall. At this point the path crosses the stream on a small stone bridge and continues down the glen.

You cross and recross the stream – there are seven bridges – before the path emerges on the narrow shingle beach of Dhoon Bay. Turn right, along the shore, to find a grassy path climbing up to your right. This doubles back across the slope and runs up the edge of the wooded glen.

You pass through a gate. Just beyond this there is a junction with another path. Go back-left here. After a few paces a path heads off to your right. Ignore this and continue across the slope, through bracken, towards the sea.

The path swings right and continues a short way to a hairpin bend, with fine views of the cliffs to the south. Double back here and follow the clear path back up the edge of the glen to reach a junction with a quiet public road.

Turn left to return to the start.

4 Cornaa & Ballaglass _____ B

A circuit through woods and farmland, past waterfalls and the shingle beach at Port Cornaa, following rough paths, tracks and quiet roads. The navigation requires a little attention in places, but this is a moderate circuit through beautiful and varied countryside. Length: **6 miles/9.5km**; *Height Climbed:* **490ft/150m**.

O.S. Sheet 95

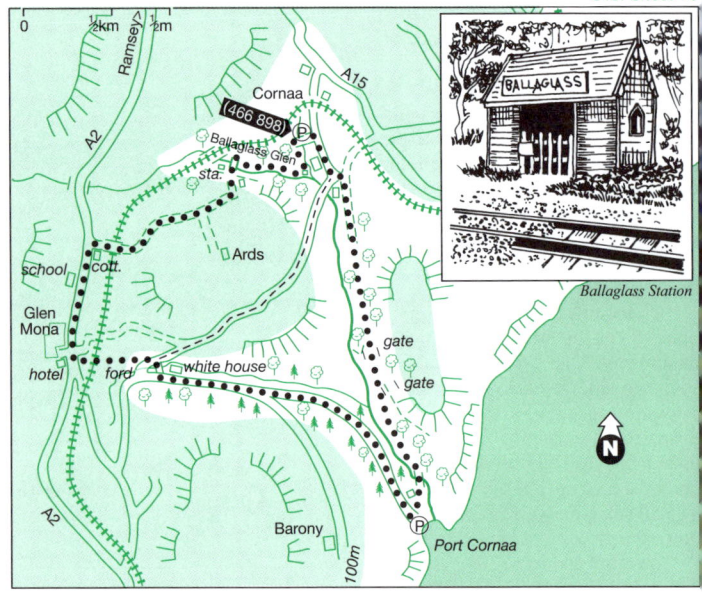

Ballaglass Station

Follow the A2 south from the centre of Ramsey for 3 miles, until you reach a junction with the A15 (signposted for Cornaa). Turn on to this road, then after a mile take the first road cutting off to the right (Cornaa). This minor road quickly crosses the railway. Park in the Ballaglass Glen car park, to the right of the road a short way beyond.

Walk on down the quiet road for a short distance. Just after passing a substantial house to your right a clear track heads off to the left, signposted for Port Cornaa (if you have followed the road over the river, you have gone too far).

Follow this rough, clear track uphill, through trees, to reach a junction with another track. Turn right here (Raad ny Foillan) and follow this descending track, ignoring paths and gates to either side. There are two significant forks in the track. At the first (where the track to the right curves down towards the river) keep left, crossing a stile beside a gate. At the second (where there is a 'private' sign on the gate to the left), keep right.

Follow the track down to a footbridge over the river, then continue down the open glen beyond to reach the car park on the raised shingle mound behind the beach at Port Cornaa.

After admiring the view, double back to your right, on the narrow access road to the car park. This climbs for a mile/1.6km, through woodland, with a narrow glen down to your right. Just after passing a white house to your right, the road begins to descend and turns to the left. At this point there is a wooden footbridge and a ford crossing the stream to your right. Cross the footbridge to join a metalled road.

Here you have a choice. If you want to shorten your walk, turn right here and follow the road (with care: it is very narrow in places) for a mile/1.6km to return to the car park. To complete the walk, simply cross the road from the end of the footbridge and follow a rough, damp path (signposted) uphill; crossing the railway then continuing for a short distance to join the A2 opposite the Glen Mona Hotel.

Turn right, following the pavement on the near side of the road. After a short distance the road passes a primary school (on the far side of the road) then begins to descend. Just beyond a white cottage ('Hillcrest') a sign points right for a footpath. Turn right here, on a clear track.

The track quickly crosses the railway, then continues for half a mile/0.8km to reach a fork. Keep left here (footpath) and follow the rough vehicle track beyond along field edges. The track eventually passes a white cottage then goes through a gate to reach a junction of paths and tracks on the edge of the wooded Ballaglass Glen.

Keep straight on here, taking a flight of steps down to the railway, visible below. Turn right on the near side of the railway to reach a further flight of steps, leading down through trees to a bridge over the river.

Cross this and turn right on a clear path. There is a mass of paths through the woods on this section. When in doubt, simply continue with the river to your right – that way you will be able to enjoy the falls and rapids in the rocky gorge.

Continue until a wooden fence starts to your right and begins to bend away from the river. Just before the left turn begins, take a path to your left, leading past a white cottage to a junction with a clear track. Walk straight across the track and follow the rough path beyond, leading up the side of a tributary stream to reach the large wooden bridge leading back across to the car park at the start.

5 Laxey Mines _____ A

A circuit through the hills above Laxey on rough tracks and footpaths passing historic points of interest. Some route finding necessary.
Length: **7¼ miles/11.5km**; *Height Climbed:* **1470ft/450m**.   O.S. Sheet 95

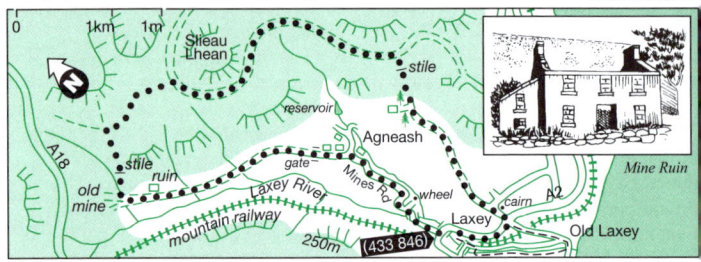

Mine Ruin

To reach the start of the walk, look for Mines Road which heads north off the main road (A2) through Laxey near the bridge over Laxey River. There is room to park to the right of the road.

Walk on up Mines Road with Laxey Wheel visible ahead. When the wheel appears down a lane ahead, keep left on the road and continue, climbing to the village of Agneash.

Shortly after you enter the village, the road splits. Look for a bridleway signposted to the left by a parking area with a post box. Follow the road with houses to the right to reach a gate. Go through this (footpath sign), now on a stony track, and follow it up the glen through a series of gates.

The track eventually reaches the ruins of the old mine. Just after passing a large ruin to the right, the track splits. Go right, then right again at a footpath sign marking the start of a narrow path. Follow this as it climbs steeply to a stile over a wall.

Cross the stile and continue straight uphill. There is no path here but occasional posts mark the way. Ignore a faint path off to the right, and climb to reach a clear 4-way junction marked by a tall post. Go right and follow a braided path as it contours the hill then drops to a wooden barrier leading to a T-junction with a clear stony track. Go right (bridleway).

Follow this track, with the small triangular reservoir above Agneash coming into view below.

As the track drops, look for a post with a red arrow ('Bike Link') to the right. Leave the track and follow a narrow path to a stile. Cross this and continue between fields, dropping towards a stand of conifers.

When the path meets a track, go left and follow it to the public road on the edge of the village. Go right at a junction to reach the main road.

A turn to the right leads back to the start. If you wish to visit Old Laxey, go straight ahead, then follow a riverside path back to the car park.

6 Kirk Michael _____ A

A steep, varied circuit, climbing on a quiet public road and rough track to a ridge, providing fine views, then returning along an old railway line.
Length: **8 miles/13km**; *Height Climbed:* **985ft/300m**.

O.S. Sheet 95

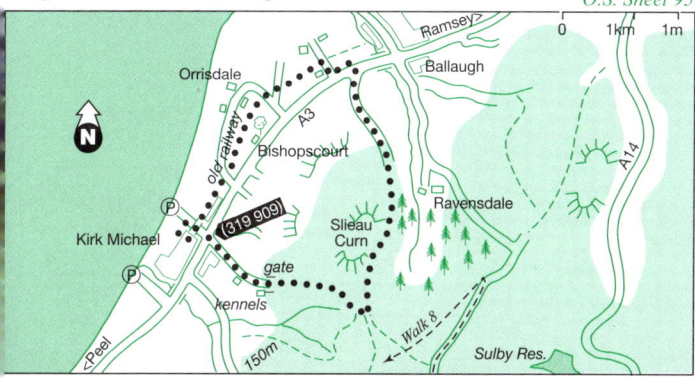

Park in Kirk Michael and look for Bayr ny Balleira (a road leading off the main street, heading towards the coast). Immediately opposite the start of this road, an unnamed road sets off between buildings (signpost for a cat home/kennel). This road leads out of the village and uphill through fields, for a mile/1.6km, until it ends at a gate/stile beyond the kennels.

Keep straight on along the clear track beyond, winding up onto the ridge between Slieau Curn and Slieau Freoaghane. Here, there is a junction with a well-rutted track. Go left, descending along the right-hand side of the ridge, with a deep wooded glen down to your right. After a little over a mile/1.6km the track re-enters fields and becomes a lane, then becomes a metalled road and descends to a junction with the A3.

Cross the road (carefully) and turn left along the pavement on the far side. After 100m an entrance road starts to your right. Turn on to this, passing a house to your left then immediately turning left along the line of the old railway.

Follow the old railway for 2½ miles/4km, passing the impressive Bishopscourt (at one time official residence of the Bishop of Sodor and Man) along the way, until you are back in Kirk Michael. As the line is sunken at this point, you may not be sure of where you are; just continue until the line crosses a sunken road on a narrow bridge. Descend to the right at the far end of the bridge, then double back under the line to follow Bayr ny Balleira back to the start.

7 Sulby_____A

A moderate circuit, climbing through farmland and woodland, running through moorland for a stretch, then descending and returning along a quiet public road. There are good views from the high section. The paths are rough and wet in places, but the route is clear. **Length: 6½ miles/10.5km**; **Height Climbed: 985ft/300m**.

O.S. Sheet 95

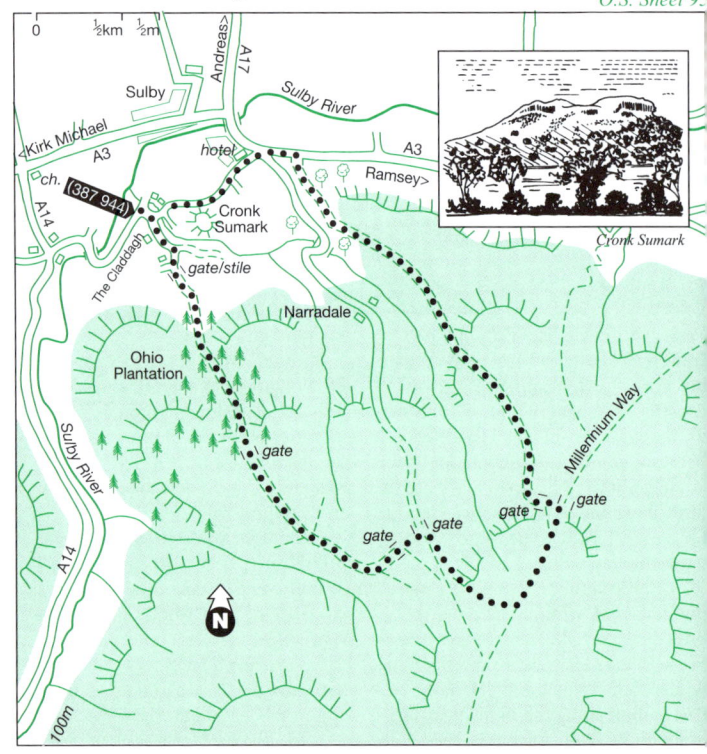

To reach the start of this route, drive 4 miles west from Ramsey on the A3. Pass through the village of Sulby. A short distance beyond, just by a church, there is a four-way junction. Turn left onto the A14. After a further short distance there is a four-way junction in a group of houses.

Turn left on the minor road to Sulby Claddagh.

The road quickly crosses Sulby River and enters a strip of common land, used for camping and recreation. Park somewhere along this grassy stretch then walk on along the road. The road enters trees and dog-legs right, with a stream to your left. After a short distance it turns left, to cross the stream. At this point keep straight on, on a metalled road signposted as a dead end.

Follow the road uphill, through scattered houses, until the tarmac ends and the road splits into two tracks. Go left (signposted as a footpath), crossing a stile by a gate then climbing a short distance further to reach the edge of the conifers of Ohio Plantation. Follow the track uphill through the trees. At the top of the wood the track heads right – still inside the wood – but you go straight on: passing through a metal gate then continuing on a clear track.

You are now climbing on a lane between gorse bushes. As you climb, the gorse becomes lower and you can see fields to either side. The track eventually swings hard left. At this point there is a stile to your right and a sign for a footpath. Ignore this and continue along the lane, which ends at a gate leading onto moorland.

Immediately beyond the gate the track splits. Keep left, following a rough track which quickly joins a wall to the left. In a short distance you reach the top of the gated lane coming up from Narradale. Ignore this and turn right. The main track through the moorland is heavily used by cyclists. To avoid this, take the fainter path to the left. This starts parallel to the main track, but gradually pulls away to the left as it climbs.

This path climbs for ½ mile/0.8km to join a well-used ridge path (part of the Millennium Way). Turn left along this, enjoying the view of the patchwork of fields below, with the northern plain of the island beyond. Follow this track for ½ mile/0.8km until it reaches a gate. Rather than going through the gate, turn left, with a wall to your right. After 100m there is a further gate. Go through this and start descending on a clear track between grassy, heathery walls.

Follow this track downhill for 2 miles/3km, noting the distinctive mound of Cronk Sumark (an obvious defensive site, with the remains of an Iron Age fort on its summit) over to your left. When you join the public road (A3), turn left along the pavement on the near side of the road. You quickly reach a complex junction of roads by the Ginger Hall Hotel. Ignore the little road to Narradale to your left, and instead go half-left (ie, leaving the hotel to your right).

The start of the walk is a little under a mile along this road. It is a quiet road, but it is narrow in places, so keep an eye open for traffic. If you are interested in climbing Cronk Sumark, watch for a sign for the start of the path to the left of the road. It is a short, steep climb, but the views are excellent.

8 Sulby Reservoir _____ B

A fine circuit through the high moors above Sulby Reservoir on clear tracks and a quiet public road. **Length:** *up to* **7½ miles/12km**; **Height Climbed:** *up to* **880ft/270m** *(on summit detour).*

O.S. Sheet 95

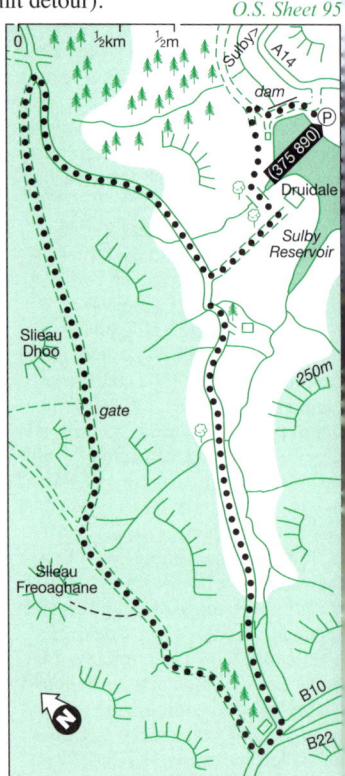

To reach the start of this walk follow the A14 south from the village of Sulby for a little under 4 miles to reach the reservoir. The car park is to the right of the road.

Drop down to cross the dam and at the far side go right, on a track, to reach a gate. Go round this. You quickly reach a junction, go left and follow a grassy path with the reservoir below to your left.

The path drops to cross a wooden footbridge at the head of the reservoir, then climbs between fields to reach the entrance drive to Druidale Farm. Go right and follow the drive up to a quiet public road.

Go right and follow the road for 1 mile/1.6km, climbing steadily. When the climb eases, look for a track cutting back to the left (bridleway). From here the route is straightforward. Follow the track as it contours around Slieau Dhoo with a wall to the left. Ignore a track joining from the right, just before a gate, and continue climbing to join another track at an acute angle. Go left. When the track levels out, a faint path heads right through heather to the summit of Slieau Freoaghane (if you reach the conifers to your left then you have missed it). A short detour to the summit gives fine views over the island.

To complete the circuit, follow the track downhill with a band of conifers to your left to reach a public road. Go left, then left again by a cottage on to a minor road. Follow this for 2 miles/3km back to the drive to Druidale Farm. Retrace your steps from here back to the car park.

9 North Barrule _____ A

A lineal ridge walk providing fine views of the northern end of the island. Paths are rough and damp in places. **Length: 6miles/9.5km**; *Total Height Climbed:* **1,440ft/440m**.

O.S. Sheet 95

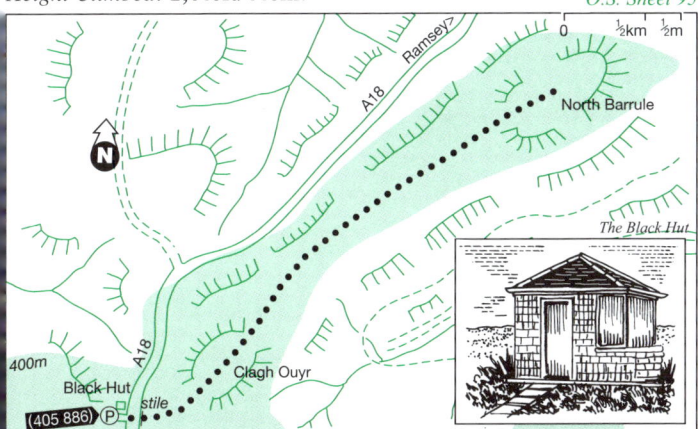

North Barrule (1842ft/561m) is the second highest peak on the Isle of Man. The actual peak is the raised end of a long ridge which heads east from the foot of Snaefell and juts out above the low land south of Ramsey. This walk follows the ridge.

To reach the start of the walk, find the junction of the A14 and the A18, 8 miles north of the centre of Douglas. The junction is marked by Bungalow Station, on the Snaefell Mountain Railway. From here, drive north on the A18, towards Ramsey. This is part of the TT course, and there is a series of huts beside the road. Park in the parking area immediately before the third of these, Black Hut.

Cross the road from the car park to find a stile and a sign for a footpath. This is the start of the walk. The path beyond is clear, if wet: starting along the line of an old wall, before edging off to the left and climbing straight to the top of the first peak – Clagh Ouyr.

Beyond this the route is simple: a 2 mile/3km ridge walk, over a series of low peaks, to reach the final peak of North Barrule. There are duckboards over a wet area on the col beyond Clagh Ouyr, but otherwise the route is straightforward. There are fine views from all along the ridge, notably northwards to Ramsey and the island's north plain, with the lighthouse at Point of Ayre visible in the distance (*see* Walk 1).

Return by the same route.

Walks Isle of Man

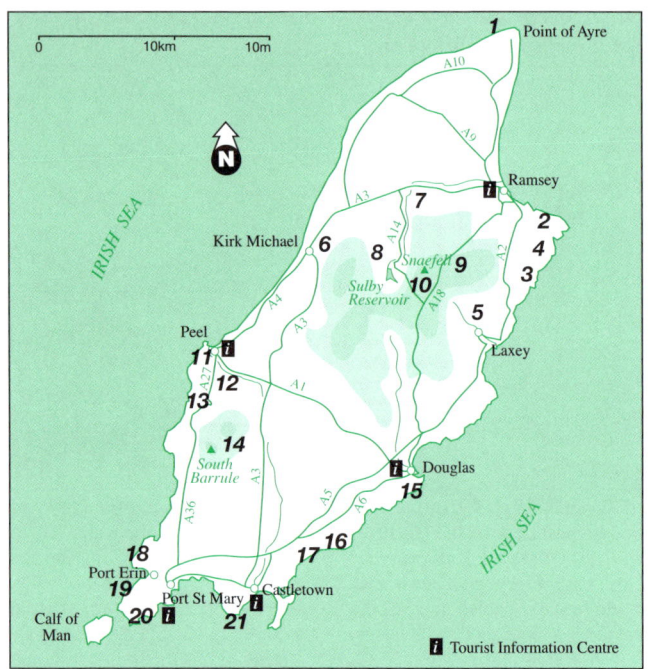

Grades

A ...... Full walking equipment and ability to navigate required

B ...... Strong walking footwear and waterproof clothing required

C ...... Comfortable walking footwear recommended

NB: Assume each walk increases at least one grade in poor weather

Walks Isle of Man

	walk	grade
1	Point of Ayre	C
2	Port Lewaigue & Maughold Head	B
3	Dhoon Glen	B
4	Cornaa & Ballaglass	B
5	Laxey Mines	A
6	Kirk Michael	A
7	Sulby	A
8	Sulby Reservoir	B
9	North Barrule	A
10	Snaefell	A
11	Peel Hill & Corrins Hill	B
12	Peel Hill, Glen Maye & St John's	A
13	Glen Maye	C
14	South Barrule	B
15	Douglas: Marine Drive	C
16	Port Grenaugh & Santon Head	B
17	Port Grenaugh & Port Soldrick	B
18	Bradda Head	A
19	Port Erin to Calf Sound	B
20	Calf Sound to Port St Mary	A
21	Scarlett Point	C

— www.pocketwalks.com —

Published by: Hallewell Publications, Scotland
Printed by: Barr Printers, Glenrothes

While every care has been taken in the preparation of this guide, the publishers cannot accept responsibility for any loss, damage or injury resulting from its use.

10 Snaefell   A

A straightforward climb to the highest point on the island, with stunning views on a clear day – however it can be cold and cloudy on the summit, so go prepared. Possibility of combining the walk with a ride on the mountain railway. Length: **1½ miles/2.5km** *(there and back); Height Climbed:* **720ft/220m**.

O.S. Sheet 95

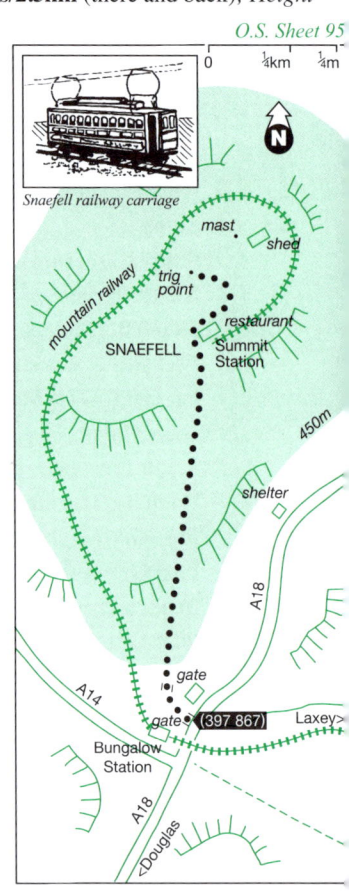

Snaefell railway carriage

Snaefell, the highest hill on the island, is easily distinguished by the large mast and cluster of buildings on its summit. This includes the restaurant for the Snaefell Mountain Railway, an electric railway that runs from Laxey to the summit (summer months only) and may provide an alternative descent or source of refreshment.

The climb can be started from various points, but the simplest ascent is from Bungalow Station, approximately 5 miles north of Douglas at the junction of the A18 and the A14. There is room to park near the station.

Look for a kissing gate ('Snaefell') at the north end of a long layby to the left of the A18. Go through this and follow the rough path beyond through a second gate. The route from here is never in doubt, with the rough path – wet and braided in places – climbing steadily to reach the end of the mountain railway.

Cross the end of this and walk up the left-hand side of the restaurant. A concrete path leads around the building and on up to the trig point and view indicator on the summit.

On a clear day you can see most of the island below and over to England, Scotland, Wales and Ireland.

Return by the same route.

11 Peel Hill & Corrins Hill _____ B

A popular circuit above the picturesque harbour town of Peel, following cliff-top paths and clear tracks. Length: **4 miles/6.5km**; *Height Climbed:* **325ft/100m**. *Possible link with Walk 12*

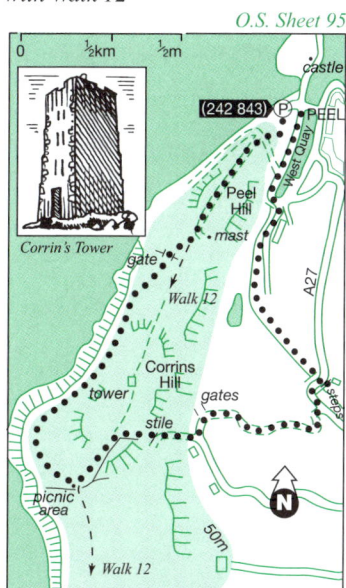

O.S. Sheet 95

Start this walk from the west side of Peel's busy harbour. Drive (or walk) to the end of West Quay to reach Fenella Beach car park – just before the causeway leading to the castle.

On the left-hand side of the entrance to the car park, a flight of steps leads on to the grassy slopes of Peel Hill. There are numerous paths and tracks on the hill. Look for a grassy path marked by benches, and follow it over the top of the hill and down to the low col before Corrins Hill.

Just before reaching a radio mast, the path splits. If you wish to visit the dramatic folly (1806) on the peak of the hill, keep straight on. Otherwise, go right on a grassy path. You quickly reach a gate in a wall. Go through this and continue on a clear path along the cliff top. As you approach the headland, the cliffs give way to fields to the right and the path converges with a wall coming in from the right. A short way along the wall you join the Raad ny Foillan. Ignore the path going through a gate to your right and continue with the wall to your right and Corrin's Tower ahead.

When the wall cuts hard right, follow it, dropping to a stile. Cross this to join a track. Go left and continue to a T-junction with a clear track, by a house. Go left along this.

The clear track ends at field gates. Go right here on a grassy path between hedges and follow this down to join a track. Go right along this and drop down to join a public road.

Cross the road to a pavement and go left to reach a bridge (careful of traffic). At the far end look for a flight of wooden steps that drops down to the right. Go down these to join a walkway along the river bank. Go left, under the road bridge, and follow the walkway by the river to the public road to the harbour. Go left at the bridge to return to the start.

12 Peel Hill, Glen Maye & St John's ———— A

An extension of Walk 11. This is a complex but varied walk, including sections along coastal cliffs, up a wooded glen, through farmland and woodland, and finally along a riverside path. Paths are of varying quality; the views and landscape excellent. **Length: 11 miles/18km**; *Height Climbed:* **1150ft/350m**, plus undulations on the coastal path.

O.S. Sheet 95

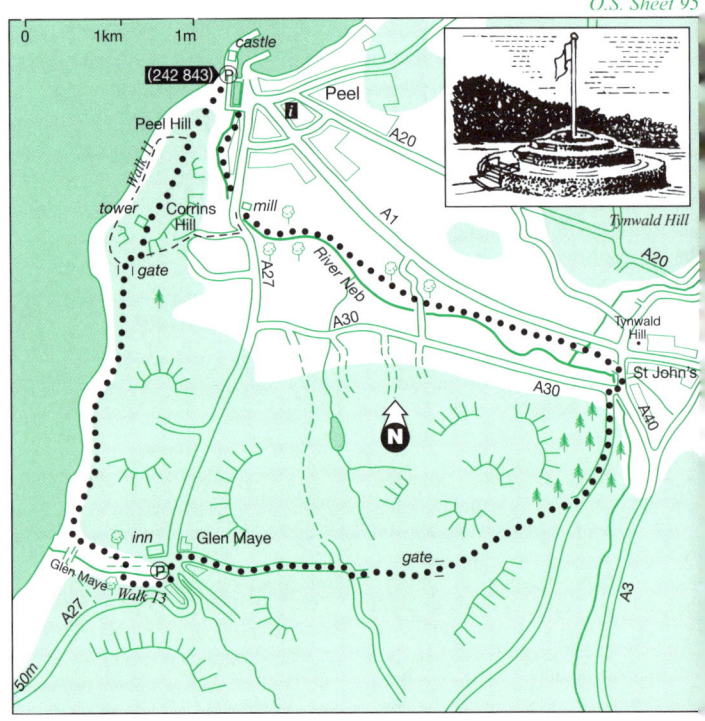

Start as for Walk 11, either following the coast path or climbing past the folly on Corrins Hill. Either way, on the far side of the hill you will reach the wall crossing the line of the route further along the cliffs. At an angle in the wall, near the cliff edge, there is a kissing-gate marked by a black arrow. Go through the gate and continue along the cliff-top path beyond.

The path is rough and potentially dangerous in places – as it runs near the top of a steep, grassy slope – but there is no doubt about the route: simply follow the cliff top for 2 miles/3km until your progress is halted by a deep, wooded glen with a shingle beach at its foot. This is Glen Maye.

The path swings left, away from the sea, along the edge of the glen. Ignore a signposted path heading back to your right (*see* Walk 13) and continue, gradually descending to join a metalled road running down the glen. On the far side of the road is a gate labelled 'entrance to glen'. Go through this and follow one of the paths through the trees and past the waterfalls up to the village of Glen Maye (*see* Walk 13).

You enter the village in the parking area in front of the Waterfall Inn. Walk up to the main road through the village (the A27) and turn left. After a short distance a dead-end road heads off to your right (Glen Rushen Road). Ignore this and take the next turn to the right (unnamed, but immediately beyond the building marked as The Old Post Office'). This narrow, metalled road quickly leaves the houses and climbs steeply as a sunken lane between fields.

Follow this road for a mile/1.6km – climbing steeply at first, then levelling out – until it dog-legs sharply to the right. At this point a signposted track heads off to the left. Ignore that and follow the road round the corner and on for a few paces, until a second track heads off to the left. Follow this track, climbing gently, until, just short of the highest point, there are twin gates ahead with tracks beyond each. Take the left-hand track.

The track descends gently for a mile/1.6km – initially through moorland, then between fields, and finally as a sunken lane through woodland – before joining a quiet public road. Go left along this (keeping out of the way of any traffic) and follow it to a junction with Patrick Road, on the edge of the village of St John's. Turn right along this to reach a T-junction, then turn left on Station Road. Walk a short distance along this road. Looking ahead you will see a large flagpole (at the site of the Tynwald Day ceremony), but for this walk turn left immediately after crossing a bridge over a river.

There is still 3 miles/5km of the walk to go, but from here the route is straightforward. It starts as a metalled road, leading to a large parking area to your right. Keep straight on at this point. You are following the line of the old Douglas-Peel railway line, so ignore any paths and tracks heading off to right or left and keep straight ahead – sometimes between fields, sometimes through woods, and increasingly with the River Neb to your left.

The path passes under a road bridge (A27) by an old mill, and continues through pleasant woodland to the outskirts of Peel. Follow the riverside path past houses and on to the head of the harbour.

13 Glen Maye

A short, steep walk following the circuit of paths through a deep, wooded glen; down to a narrow shingle beach and back past a fine waterfall.
Length: **2 miles/3km**; *Height Climbed:* **260ft/80m**.

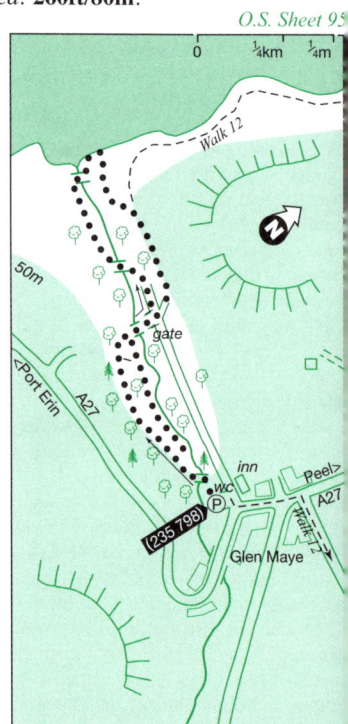

To reach Glen Maye village, drive 2½ miles south from Peel on the A27. There is a car park in front of the Waterfall Inn for the use of inn patrons and those visiting the glen.

Take the path to the left of the toilet block. A flight of steps leads down to a picnic area and a bridge. At the far end of the bridge the track splits. Keep to the left (the other path is your return route), descending through fine mixed woodland with the deep glen down to your right. As you approach the end of the path, two paths head off to your right (the second signposted for the waterfall). Ignore these for the moment and follow the path over the river and up to a gate leading on to a quiet public road.

Turn left and follow the road (it quickly becomes a track) out of the trees and down to the shingle beach at the foot of the glen. Cross a footbridge over the river. Just beyond, there is a ruined stone shelter set against the cliff. Just beyond this, turn right on a rough, steep path climbing the grassy slope. Follow this up to a junction with a clearer path (Walk 12) and turn right.

The path brings you back down to the public road immediately opposite the entrance to the glen. Start back up your original path, but this time keep left at the sign for the waterfall and follow a sequence of paths and steps (slippy in places, so take care) into the heart of the deep glen, where there is a fine viewpoint for the waterfall. The path then climbs to rejoin your original path at the junction noted before.

14 South Barrule _____ B

A short, lineal hill climb leading to a splendid viewpoint – choose a day when the top is clear. The path is rough, and damp in places, but there is no doubt about the route. Length: **1½ miles/2.5km**; *Height Climbed:* **590ft/180m**.

O.S. Sheet 95

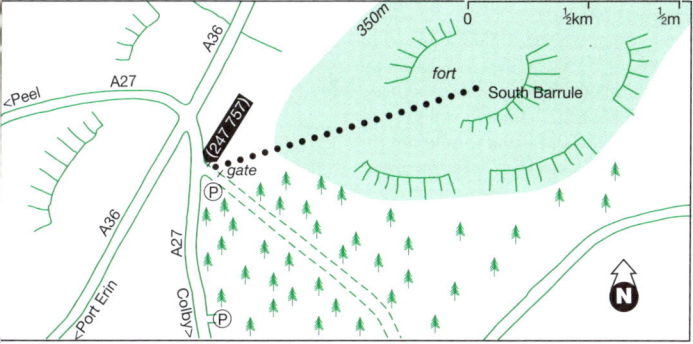

South Barrule is not particularly high – 1585ft/483m – but it is the highest peak in the south of the island, which makes it a fine viewpoint, and the rough moorland gives it the feel of a higher hill. In folklore, it was long believed to be the home of Manannan – the Celtic sea god who may have given the island its name.

To reach it, drive 5 miles north from Port Erin on the A36 to reach the four-way junction with the A27. Turn right here (ie, on the road to Colby). After a very short distance a plantation of conifers starts to the left of the road, and a rough track heads off ahead-left, with the trees to its right. There is room for a few cars to park beside the end of this track. (If there is no room here, drive a further ½ mile along the road and park in the car park in the trees to the left of the road, then walk back along the road.)

Just at the point where the track leaves the road there is a sign for a footpath, pointing through a kissing-gate, with a clear path beyond, climbing through the heather.

There is no possible doubt about the route – just keep walking uphill. At the top you will find the remains of an Iron Age fort (this appears to have been the main defensive site in the south of the island from earliest times) and, weather permitting, you should get some fine views. You should certainly be able to see down to the southern end of the island, and on a clear day may be able to see as far as the coasts of Ireland, Scotland, England and Wales.

Return by the same route.

15 Douglas: Marine Drive

An easy there-and-back walk on tarred roads from Douglas, with superb views over the town. Possible extension up a small glen. Length: up to **9 miles/14.5km** (there and back); Height Climbed: **325ft/100m**.

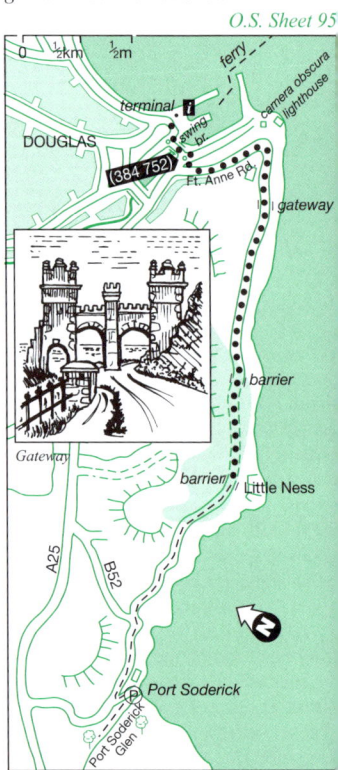

Start from the ferry terminal in Douglas and look for a sign for the A5 Castletown road. This leads over the swing bridge at the entrance to the inner harbour to a roundabout. On the far side of this there is a flight of steps. Climb these and turn left at the top along a road (Fort Anne Road) lined by handsome stone houses.

The road leaves the houses behind and a fine view opens up over an area of parkland to the left, down to the harbour. Pass the entrance to the Camera Obscura on your left and continue along the road to reach the large ornate stone gateway to Marine Drive. Continue beyond the gateway. The pavement ends, but there is a path by the side of the road.

After a further mile/1.6km you reach a barrier across the road. Cars are not allowed along the next section but the road continues as a footpath along the cliffs.

Continue, passing a further vehicle barrier by the viewpoint at Little Ness, noting the amazing rock formations in the cliffs below the road.

It is simplest just to return from here, but if you wish a longer walk, continue to a junction with a public road. Go left (Raad ny Foillan) and drop down to the small car park for Soderick Glen at the end of the road.

A short, pleasant path leads up the glen, crossing and re-crossing the river. It is also possible to make a short detour to visit the old beach resort at Port Soderick. Return by the same route.

16 Port Grenaugh & Santon Head _____ B

A short circuit from the small inlet of Port Grenaugh, out along a clifftop path and returning along rough paths and lanes. Length:
3½ miles/5.5km; *Height Climbed:* **230ft/70m**.

O.S. Sheet 95

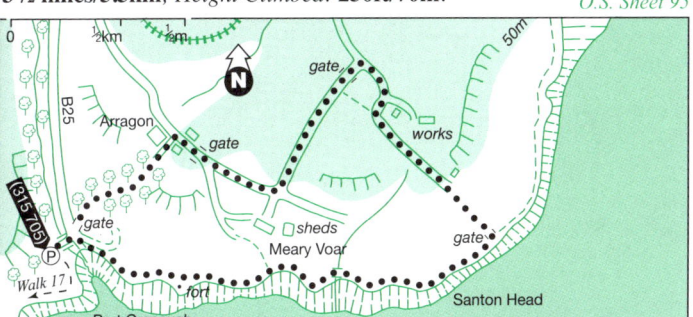

To reach Port Grenaugh, drive south from Douglas on the A6. After around one mile the A25 cuts off to the left. Follow this for a little over 4 miles then turn left on the B25, signposted for Port Grenaugh. There is a car park at the end of the road.

Walk back out of the car park and go right, passing a footpath sign (this is your return route) and follow the blue sign for the Raad ny Foillan. The path climbs steeply at first, crosses a metal rail stile, and quickly reaches the remains of an iron age fort. Explore the ruins, taking care not to stray too close to the cliff edge.

The path continues along the cliffs, dropping to cross two footbridges. Just beyond the second a large house appears to the left and a footpath sign points left. It is possible to shorten your route here (*see* map), but for this walk continue along the coast.

Just beyond Santon Head, a second footpath heads left. Follow this through a gate. The going beyond is rough, with fences to either side, but you quickly join a metalled track. Go straight ahead and follow the track around the sewage works. Beyond the entrance, look for a footpath sign pointing left, down a tarred driveway. Follow this, crossing a stile to the right of a large gate (Meary Voar) and continuing beyond.

As you approach the house, go right (sign) heading for a second gate. Cross the stile here and follow the road beyond, dropping down towards Arragon House. Go left just before the house (sign), through a kissing gate and on down a tree-lined grass path. Follow the footpath signs and, when you reach a gravel path, go left and follow it through a delightful narrow glen to return to the car park.

17 Port Grenaugh & Port Soldrick _____ B

A complex circuit, starting along clifftops and returning by paths, tracks and a quiet public road. Length: **4½ miles/7km**; *Height Climbed:* up to **310ft/95m**.

O.S. Sheet 95

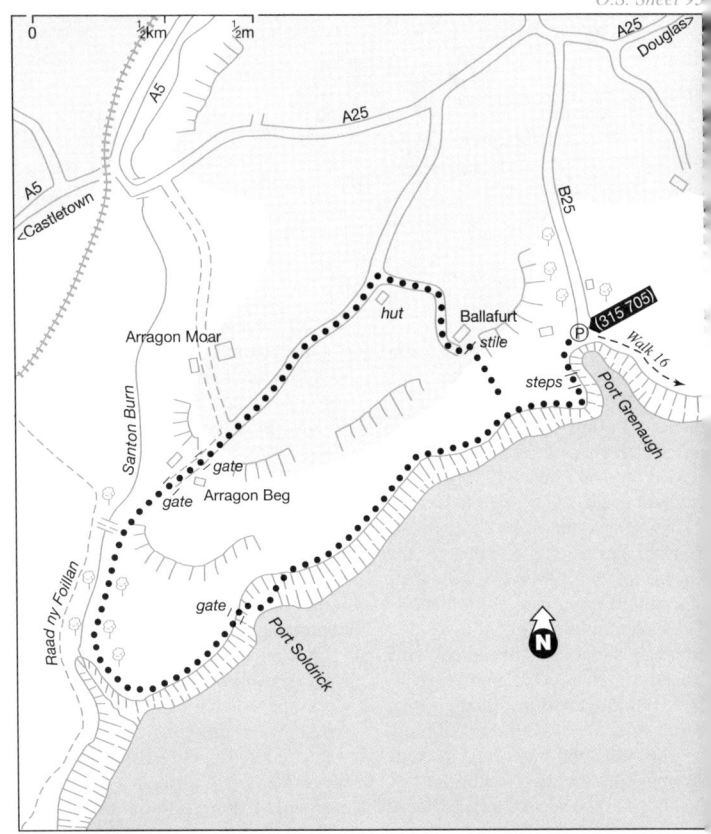

To reach the start of this route, follow the directions given for Walk 16. From the road end at Port Grenaugh, head right along the head of the narrow beach to reach a flight of steps leading up to the top of the low cliff. Here, a path continues along the coast, with the slanting grassy cliffs leading down to the sea to your left. After a short distance there is a signposted junction, with a path heading off to the right. This is your return route; for now, keep straight on.

The path runs along the rough ground outside the cliff-top fields. Occasionally, where there is insufficient room, a gate leads through the fence to your right and you walk along the foot of the field for a short distance. Where this happens, keep close to the fence and watch for the gate leading back on to the clifftop.

After a mile/1.6km the path reaches the deep inlet of Port Soldrick. Here, the path edges down the slope to run along the head of a beach before climbing back to the cliff top at the far side of the bay. (At the time of writing, parts of this path are badly eroded: take care and follow any instructions given on the ground.)

Once you are back on the cliff top there is a gate, beyond which the path continues. Looking ahead there is a fine view of the hammerhead peninsula of Langness and the built-up end of the runway at Isle of Man Airport.

The path swings right, up the side of a narrow inlet lined with gorse. Continue until you reach a gate leading into a field. A sign for the Raad ny Foillan points straight on, so now you are walking up the edge of the field with a bank of gorse to your left. After a very short distance a sign points left, into a wood of hawthorn and oak. You are now on a grassy path – occasionally duckboards – running up a wooded glen with the little stream to your left.

Continue until you reach a stile over a fence to your left, and a signpost pointing left towards a footbridge over the Santon Burn. That is the coast path, but for this walk keep straight on, with the fence to your left. After a few paces you pass a post with a green arrow on it.

Continue to reach a gate, beyond which you are on a track – still with a fence to your left. Within a short distance this leads to the ruined buildings at Arragon Beg. Pass between these, go through a gate, and continue up the track beyond to reach the end of a metalled road with grass down the middle.

Walk straight up this (ie, ignoring the entrance to the cylindrical mansion at Arragon Moar to your left). After ½ mile/0.8km you pass a hut to the right of the road, just beyond which a metalled entrance road heads off to the right, signposted as a footpath and for Ballafurt.

Turn on to this track, which climbs briefly then descends to pass to the right of the buildings at Ballafurt. The garden below the buildings to your left ends and the track curves left to pass below it. At this point there is a stile directly ahead of you and a sign for a footpath.

Cross the stile and take the path straight down the field edge ahead to rejoin your original path at the junction noted before. Turn left to return to the start.

18 Bradda Head _____ A

A terrific coast walk, passing a dramatic hilltop folly and providing superb views. The paths are rough and steep in places, and care needs to be taken near the cliff edge. Length: **4½ miles/7km**; *Height Climbed:* up to **755ft/230m**.

From the front at Port Erin, the dramatic Milner's Tower (1871) is clearly visible. This walk passes the tower then continues along the cliffs beyond. It is possible to drive to the car park at the start of the walk (drive north from the Promenade and look for the sign pointing left to Bradda Glen – the car park is by the restaurant), but if you wish to extend your walk it is worth starting from the Promenade. Look for a path through the grassy area in front of the Promenade, starting at a white metal barrier, and follow a sequence of dramatic paths along the low, rocky cliffs to the car park.

Walk on beyond the car park (Coronation Footpath). The path splits twice – either way will do, the paths rejoin. Continue along the coast until a sign points right for Milner's Tower. Climb to a gate in a wall running along the slope, then turn left beyond this to reach the tower (built in 1871).

Most people will simply turn back at this point, but the rest of the walk – though quite tough – is worth the effort. Simply follow the Raad ny Foillan on along the coast (the views back to the tower and the Calf of Man beyond are terrific). The path – rough but clear – continues for 1½ miles/2.5km, eventually dropping steeply, with a conifer plantation to its right, to reach a junction with a track.

A turn to the left at this point leads down to the public road, where a short walk to your left leads down to the car park behind Fleshwick Bay. Alternatively, **turn to the right** and follow the track for ½ mile/0.8km to join the A32 just north of Port Erin and the start of the walk.

19 Port Erin to Calf Sound _____ B

A dramatic section of the Raad ny Foillan, from the busy holiday village of Port Erin to the tidal narrows of Calf Sound. Length: **2 miles/3km** *(one way); Height Climbed:* **400ft/120m**. *Possible link with Walk 20.*

O.S. Sheet 95

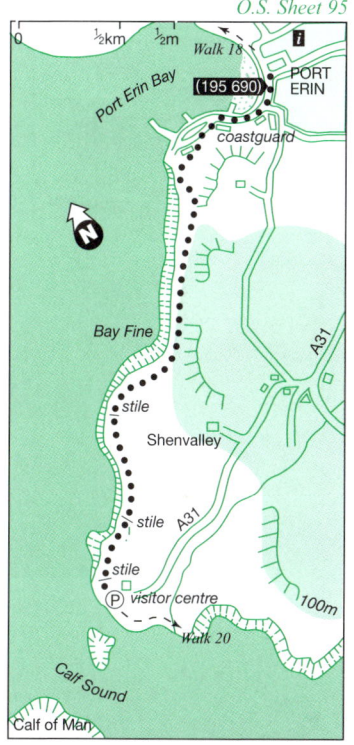

Port Erin, with its long sandy beach, is a popular holiday destination in the south-west of the island. From the centre of the village, drive or walk south along the back of the beach. (There is room to park at the end of the road beyond the harbour.)

Just beyond the Coastguard building, the road splits. Go left, on the upper road, and look for a sign for the Raad ny Foillan immediately to the left of a large red brick building. The narrow path climbs steeply behind the building at first. As you climb, with a fence now to the left and wall to the right, the view over the harbour opens up to your right.

You reach a kissing gate. Go through this and follow the wall to your left, with views now to the east. The route from here is clear, following an obvious path around the headland of Bay Fine, with the noise from Port Erin soon fading and the Calf of Man appearing ahead.

When a wall crosses the way look for a ladder stile above the coast and cross this. Beyond a second stile the path splits. Keep right, dropping to scramble round a rocky headland.

When a broken wall comes in from the left, keep parallel to the shore. There is no path here, but you should soon pick up a clear path which drops down to reach a ladder stile by the Café and Visitor Centre car park. Refreshments are available here while you enjoy the view of the turbulent tide through the narrows.

Either return by the same route or continue along the coast on Walk 20.

20 Calf Sound to Port St Mary _____ A

A lineal cliff-top walk on rough footpaths. The path is steep and undulating, but the views are terrific. Care needs to be taken when near the cliff edge. Length: **5¹/₂ miles/9km**; *Total Height Climbed:* **560ft/170m**. *Possible link with Walk 19.*

O.S. Sheet 95

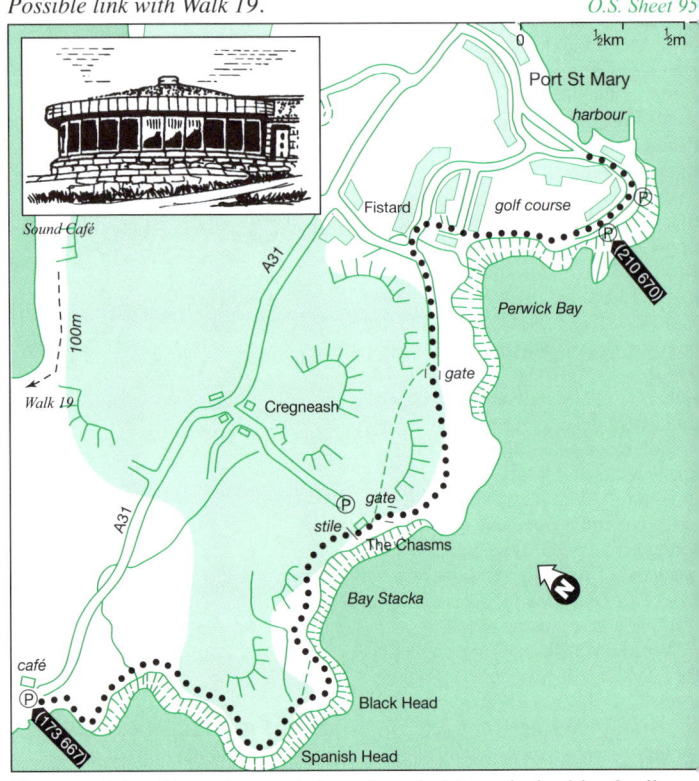

If you are doing this route as part of a walk around the south-west headland of the island, then start at Port Erin and follow Walk 19 to the café and visitor centre overlooking Calf Sound. Alternatively, drive 2 miles south from Port St Mary on the A31 and park in the car park looking over the sound to the heathery mound of Calf of Man.

Walk out the front of the car park and turn left (ie, with the sea to your right). There is a mass of paths at first, but this is quickly reduced to a single path around the head of a rocky inlet. On the far side of the inlet, cross a stile and walk along the bottom of a field for a short distance before a further stile takes you back to the rough ground above the cliffs. At a second inlet you make a similar diversion across the corner of a field. Beyond that, the path is more straightforward, climbing, through moorland, up to and along the cliffs of the massive headland of Spanish Head.

Behind the headland the path splits. The right-hand path makes a detour around Black Head; the left-hand path cuts off the corner. They rejoin beyond the headland and continue around Bay Stacka.

On the far side of the bay the path reaches a stile over a wall, with a disused two-storey building beyond. In front of the building (now maintained as a shelter) there is a gate and a sign for 'The Chasms': a network of deep, narrow gashes in the adjacent cliffs. They are a dramatic sight, but should be approached with caution.

Return to the building. Beyond it, there is a sign pointing straight on for a footpath, and another pointing right for the Raad ny Foillan. Take the latter and follow a rough path downhill to reach a gate in a wall, leading into a field.

Go through the gate and head half-left to reach an obvious signpost on the side of the field. This marks the start of a walled lane between fields. The walls soon end, but the route continues as a grassy track through a sequence of fields. This ends at a gate leading on to the end of a well-used lane. Follow this (it quickly becomes a metalled road) down into the little village of Fistard.

Amongst the houses there is a fork in the road. Go right (Port St Mary). The road descends to cross a small stream, then starts to climb again. Just at this point a sign points right for the coastal path. Go through a gap in a wall and along behind a cottage before emerging on the road through a development of new houses.

Walk along the pavement to the right of the road. At a junction, ignore a road heading off to the left. Just beyond that, when the road swings left, there is a sign pointing right for the coastal path. Go through a gate and walk on, with a wall and a house to your left, and the shrub-covered slope leading down to the shore to your right.

In a short distance, this path leads to a gate leading on to the end of Clifton Road. There is a car park near the end of the road – marked by four flagpoles – if someone is picking you up. Otherwise, continue along the road to reach the harbour and the centre of the town. If you have started from Port Erin, then it is possible to walk back along the public roads. It is not great walking, however, and on balance, it is probably better to take one of the frequent buses linking the two towns.

21 Scarlett Point   C

A lineal coastal path, giving fine views. The path is rough in places, but there is no doubt about the route. Length: **4½ miles/7km** there and back; *Height Climbed:* negligible.   *O.S. Sheet 95*

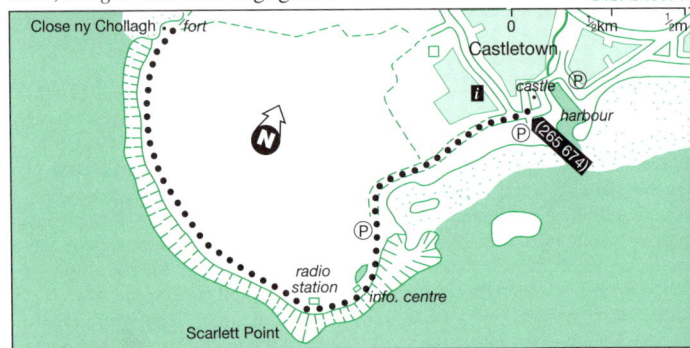

Castletown is a handsome harbour town in the south of the island. It was the island's capital until 1869, and has a fine 13th/16th-century castle.

It is possible to start at the car park at the start of the walk, but for the full walk park in one of the town's car parks and make for the Market Square, to the south-west of the massive Castle Rushen. At the square's south-west corner (ie, at the end towards the sea), a brown sign for Scarlett Point points along Queen St.

Follow the street along the front – initially with houses to the right, then on along the coast, to end at a small car park. Continue along a clear track along the coast, initially with a pool in an old quarry to your right. After a short distance you pass an information centre with information on the area's geology and wildlife.

Beyond this you continue along the coast with a wall to your right and fields beyond. You pass the Scarlett Point ham radio station at the most southerly point, then the coast bends round to the north, giving fine views over to Calf of Man and Port St Mary.

Continue as far as Close ny Chollagh, just before a quarry (note the low, grassy mounds of an Iron Age fort to your left), then return by the same route.

1 *Chicken Rock Lighthouse* **2** *Calf of Man* **3** *Spanish Head* **4** *Port St Mary* **5** *Milner's Tower, Bradda Head*